SEASONS

WHAT I SEE IN FALL

by Danielle J. Jacks

TABLE OF CONTENTS

Words to Know. 2

What I See in Fall. 3

Let's Review!. 16

Index. 16

tadpole books

WORDS TO KNOW

apples

coats

costumes

leaves

pumpkins

school bus

WHAT I SEE IN FALL

It is fall!

It gets colder.

coat

We wear coats.

Leaves fall.

rake

We rake.

apple

Apples grow.

8

I eat one. Yum!

I see a school bus.

We go to school!

pumpkin

I see pumpkins.

We carve them!

I see costumes.

Trick or treat!

LET'S REVIEW!

What are these kids doing in fall?

INDEX

apples 8

carve 13

coats 5

costumes 14

leaves 6

pumpkins 12

rake 7

school 11